1. *Paper flower wreaths, church of Xocchel, Yucatán.*

Mexican Churches

Eliot Porter & Ellen Auerbach

Essay by Donna Pierce

University of New Mexico Press, Albuquerque

Plates 8, 10, 12, 18, 21, 25, 37, 41, 47, 48, 49, 54,
65, 66, 73, 74, 75, 79, 80, and 81 are by Ellen Auerbach.
All other plates are by Eliot Porter.

Library of Congress Cataloging-in-Publication Data

Porter, Eliot, 1901–
Mexican churches.

1. Mexico—Description and travel—1951–1980—Views.
2. Churches, Catholic—Mexico—Pictorial works.
3. Church decoration and ornament—Mexico—Pictorial
works. 4. Catholic Church—Mexico—History—Pictorial
works. 5. Mexico—Church history. I. Auerbach,
Ellen, 1906– . II. Pierce, Donna. III. Title.
F1216.P67   1987   726'.5'0972   87-13765
I S B N   0–8263–1023–0

Second printing, 1988

✠ Contents ✠

✠ *Preface* ✠

Ellen Auerbach and Eliot Porter

The photo excursion to Mexico in the fall of 1955 was suggested by Eliot Porter, who, during a short visit in 1951, had been greatly stimulated by the mixture of Spanish and Indian culture in the churches. The beautiful interiors had been little photographed and never to any extent in color, probably because of the technical difficulties involved.

We were equipped with a sketchy knowledge of Spanish and a variety of cameras (two 35mm, two 2¼ reflex, and two 4×5 view cameras plus a 16mm movie camera). The trip lasted four and a half months and covered territory from Nogales to San Cristóbal de las Casas. We traveled over 10,000 miles by Chevrolet Carryall and 1,000 miles by plane, train, taxi, and bus to Yucatán and Chiapas.

We had visited literally hundreds of churches, some for minutes, others for days. We also photographed markets, pyramids, temples, ruins, and some landscapes. Over 3,000 pictures were taken, most of them in color. Almost all the interiors were taken on 35mm color film, and Eliot Porter made the dye-transfer prints.

It is one of the uses of modern photography to make exhaustive statistical records. Flashlights and fast films facilitate the process. In our collection we rarely considered this aspect. Our only goal was to get pictures which show the saints and their surroundings as they are revered by the Mexican people. Therefore, we decided to use only the existing illumination, however dim and unsuitable it seemed from a photographic viewpoint. I saw more and more how important it was not to use additional light. The candles or colored glass were imperative in creating the atmosphere we wanted to retain. To have shed light on it would be like photographing the dawn with flashbulbs. We needed very long exposures. Tripods had to be used, and few "candid shots" were possible. Often the exposure meter showed no reaction at all, and we literally worked in the dark. But, because photofilm can accumulate light through time, some of the resulting pictures show more than met the eye. This method meant a great effort in time and patience, but it seemed the only way to catch some of the atmosphere and essence of what we saw. Permission had to be obtained to take pictures; this was often a major obstacle, especially in Indian village churches. Often we had to prevent the Indians from "prettying up" the altars.

Our pictures were not taken methodically. We would go through a church and photograph what we "liked." Often we felt attracted to the same images and divided the work. At other times different things appealed to us, and we took pictures of our choice.

The number of churches and chapels and their saints is so staggering that we were frustrated by the feeling of not having even scratched the surface, and yet this limited collection of photographs already is something of a historical record; some of the churches were being renovated even while we were taking pictures in them.

Mexico is being industrialized at a rapid pace, its highways extended and improved, the people presented with the mixed blessings of modern living. Most prefer store-bought things to their own handicrafts. More and more the hand-carved images with their homemade clothes are replaced by stereotyped plaster saints. Old floors are being ripped out and loud-patterned machine-made tiles put in their place. This change is more rapid in the north. In less prosperous, less accessible villages the changes come more slowly. There the Indians have worshipped the saints in semipagan rites for a long time. They clothe and decorate them for fiestas, but even the local priest often may know little of their history and significance.

— Ellen Auerbach, New York City

Not until I moved to Santa Fe in 1946 did I have any desire to visit Mexico. Before that, with the exception of trips to Europe, the focus of my interest was the exploration of the United States — many regions which at that time were still not as completely known as they are today. When Stieglitz exhibited my photographs in New York, I met Georgia O'Keeffe, who soon after moved to New Mexico. She established herself as a painter of the New Mexico landscape at Ghost Ranch, where I saw her frequently, and we became friends. A mutual friend was the Taos writer and poet Spud Johnson, who had accompanied D. H. Lawrence to Mexico. In February 1951, my wife, Aline, proposed a trip to Mexico for a few weeks to see a different country and to escape the last of winter. She sought Spud's advice, and together they approached Georgia, who had never been outside the United States, with the proposal that the four of us go on a trip to Mexico. It was an adventure that appealed to Georgia.

Early in February we set off from Santa Fe in separate cars for Laredo, Texas, where we crossed the border into Mexico. At a leisurely pace we followed the Pan American highway south, resting for picnic lunches on food that Georgia provided and stopping early for the night. We traveled together until we reached Mexico City, where we became separated while looking for hotel accommodations. After a few days in Mexico City, Aline and I headed south for Oaxaca.

It was in Oaxaca that I had my introduction to Mexican cathedrals and village churches and saw for the first time the naive iconology and colorful decorations that expressed simple Indian reverence. Although I spent more time photographing the Zapotec ruins at Monte Alban and Mitla than the churches in Oaxaca, it was the beauty of the Christian symbolism that in the end attracted me the most. On the way home we stopped at Yanhuitlán, an isolated, lonely monument to classical architecture, which displayed a mixture of formal and unsophisticated symbols of the Christian religion. Yanhuitlán confirmed my desire to return someday to record more generally this aspect of Mexican church art.

Aline had long felt the isolation of New Mexico from the contemporary art world and decided to spend the winter of 1955–56 in New York, where she could be in closer contact with modern, creative trends in art. This provided me with the opportunity to fulfill my goal to photograph Mexican churches. I described the idea to Ellen Auerbach, a New York photographer friend, who liked the proposal and agreed to work with me on the project. We crossed the border into Mexico at Nogales, Arizona, on December 2, 1955. In our Chevrolet van we had large amounts of film and photographic equipment, which according to a Mexican customs inspector exceeded the allowable limit for tourists; but for a consideration of twenty dollars, he said he would overlook the restriction. As we left he wished us a happy trip. We followed Route 15 down the west coast of Mexico to Tepic, where it turned eastward to Guadalajara. Our first stop was Hermosillo, where we made a short side trip to Alamo, a gloomy mining town in which the cemetery was a sight of especially macabre interest, with the tombs stacked on top of one another above the rocky ground. From Hermosillo south to Tepic we found little to attract us photographically, except at Mazatlán, so we covered the distance rapidly. Tepic, with its cathedral and other churches, was much more interesting, and we stayed there for three days before driving on to Guadalajara. We had now entered older districts of Mexico, where the mixture of Spanish and Indian cultures was more evident. Here we stayed for five days, photographing churches, street scenes, markets, and even school children. We had never intended to limit our work to churches but to take advantage of all photographic opportunities, especially those involving people.

San Miguel de Allende was our next objective, from which we visited San Miguel Viejo, the Tirados Ranch church (a short drive from Guanajuato in the center of the silver-mining district), and Atotonilco, famous for its silver chapel from which the silver had been stripped during the revolution by a local leader to pay his followers. From Atotonilco we drove to Querétaro, where we photographed the golden door, pulpit, and confessional in the church of Santa Rosa. On Christmas night the hotel roof was a good place to watch the celebration that enveloped the steeple of the church on the plaza in a blazing display of fireworks. On the way to Mexico City we stopped in Morelia for the six days of Christmas festivities. From Mexico City we went north to Acolman and to see the Teotihuacán pyramids and Aztec ruins. We also explored the country east of Mexico City around Tlaxcala and Cholula, renowned for its hundreds of churches of which Huejotzingo and Santa María Tonantzintla are among the most celebrated.

To escape the exceptional January cold that had settled on Mexico and had people talking about the *hielo* (the snow), it seemed a good idea to go to the Yucatán and return to central Mexico in spring. We drove to Veracruz on the Gulf Coast, visiting Jalapa and other towns on the way. From Veracruz we continued along the coast to Minatitlán and Coatzacoalcos, where we stored the Chevrolet in a garage. Then on January 26 we flew in a small plane to Mérida with intermediate stops at Villahermosa, Ciudad del Carmen, and Campeche. A hired car with a driver took us to all the places we wanted to see, which included several small towns and villages — of which Izamal, Hoctún, and Muna were the most interesting — and, of course, the Mayan ruins at Chichen Itzá and Uxmal. The Mayan ruins at Palenque in the tropical forest of Chiapas also interested us; they were accessible only by the railroad connecting Campeche with Coatzacoalcos. We took the bus to Campeche to catch the "Rápido" for Palenque, a name that implied a speed that was not born out by the actual performance of the train, which chugged along at fifteen to twenty miles an hour. It took all day to cover the 200 kilometers to Palenque, but judging by the wavy condition of the tracks, if a higher speed had been attempted, the train most probably would have derailed.

The Palenque ruins had been partly cleared of the tropical vegetation that was slowly destroying them, and we were able to climb down into the recesses of one of the temples, where the sacrificial chacmool was still to be seen. The "Rápido" carried us back to Coatzacoalcos, where we repossessed our car. There the greedy proprietor of a lodging house overcharged us, and when we refused to pay, called the police, who accepted our account of the dispute and fined the proprietor. After driving across the isthmus of Mexico to Tehuantepec, where a matriarchal society was clearly manifest in the markets, we continued on to Salina Cruz on the Pacific coast and Ixtepec on the Pan American highway, which went east to Ocozocoautla, Chiapa de Corzo, and San Cristóbal de las Casas in the state of Chiapas.

On February 8 we arrived in San Cristóbal, at the time of fiestas and dances at the Chamula and Tenejapa Indian villages, of which the fire dance at Chamula was the most spectacular. In an alleged hypnotic state the Indians walked barefoot and painlessly on a bed of hot coals. I noticed, however, that they all wore thick, rubber sandals. We stayed in San Cristóbal eight days, first visiting Santo Domingo, the most ornate and richly embellished of its churches. I also explored the surrounding country with an American expatriate guide, who took me to several remote Spanish and Indian villages, including that of the shy Lacandones, who are so reduced in numbers that siblings marry.

From February 18 to March 15 we stayed in Oaxaca; this was the longest time in one place of the entire trip. There are many churches in Oaxaca, of which Santo Domingo is the most famous, but we also spent a lot of time in the markets, where I was pelted one day with peppers by a vegetable vendor, who did not want to be photographed. We spent many days driving around the neighborhood of Oaxaca to villages in which the smallest churches often contained beautifully appareled images of the saints and exquisite representations of biblical events. Especially notable were the churches in San Felipe, Huitzo, Coyotepec, Matatlán, and Xoxocotlán. In the Santa Helena church in Xoxocotlán we photographed a red-haired saint, a striking feature for a Latin country. In the Coyotepec church the saints were clothed with loving and lavish care, and even though we asked the priest for permission to photograph them, which he willingly gave us, when we returned the next day, we were confronted by members of the congregation who refused to let us photograph in the church, although we said the priest had given us permission. "He does not own the church," they said, "we do." After pleading with them and expressing admiration for the beauty of the images, they relented, permitting us to photograph a few selected saints. While we were going about it, they watched to make sure we did not cheat. We also went farther afield to the earthquake-ruined church of Cuilapan and to Yanhuitlán, and, of course, we could not resist spending time in the pre-Columbian ruins of Mitla and Monte Alban.

On the last return to Mexico City we stayed in the vicinity of Puebla for a week, photographing many of the churches in the Cholula area that we had visited only briefly two months before on the way to Veracruz. As a final digression we drove to Córdoba on the southern highway to Veracruz. We arrived in Mexico City during Easter week, when religious services were being conducted in all the churches, and we witnessed the Easter service in Acolman on the first of April. At Tepotzotlán we spent a long time photographing the golden interior of the church. From Mexico City we made excursions to Cuernavaca and to Pachuca, where we visited Atotonilco el Grande and watched a Judas pageant in front of the church.

Our Mexican journey was drawing to a close, but before heading north and home, there was one part of Mexico we still wanted to see. After driving west through Morelia to Pátzcuaro, where the lake fishermen are more interested in displaying their nets to tourists than in catching fish, we went south to Uruapan, which we had been told was of special interest because of its isolated location. On the way back to Morelia we stopped to see the Templo de Jesús in Naranja. The last place in which we stopped to photograph was Zacatecas on the highway north from Morelia. Here, in a deserted monastery and national monument, I found a beautiful, blue, sculptured Guadalupe fresco — my last photograph. By now we had traveled several thousand miles throughout Mexico, had visited hundreds of chapels and churches, and had taken thousands of photographs; we were eager to leave Mexico. We took the shortest route north through Aguascalientes, Durango, and Chihuahua to El Paso and home.

— Eliot Porter, Santa Fe

✠ *Portraits of Faith* ✠

Donna Pierce

Through the centuries the churches of Mexico have served their communities as true sanctuaries — places of quiet refuge for personal communion with saints and places of public worship for the reaffirmation of shared beliefs. The most important events of a person's life in Mexico take place in the church setting: baptism, confirmation, marriage, funeral, and communal celebrations, as well as, for many Mexicans, the daily ritual of mass. The churches of Mexico provide visual testimony to the changes in cultural and political thought, aesthetics, and even economic conditions over the centuries.

In their portraits of saints, Porter and Auerbach have captured the spirituality of the Mexican people. Although few humans are visible in the photographs, their presence is felt and their devotion to the saints is apparent. These photographs serve not only as portraits of saints, but also as portraits of faith.

The introduction of Christianity to Mexico dates to the early sixteenth century, and the epic saga of the Conquest of Mexico has all the ingredients of great drama. Hernán Cortés and his band of men, one ocean and thousands of miles from home, arrived in the New World with religious and patriotic fervor still fresh from the recent Reconquest of Spain. After more than seven hundred years of Moslem domination, the Spanish Christians, united under King Ferdinand and Queen Isabella, had finally evicted the Moors from Spanish soil in 1492. The discovery of the New World in the same year that the Moors were evicted from Spain was interpreted by Spanish ecclesiastics and laymen alike as a sign from God. They considered themselves chosen by God to spread the word of Christ to the thousands of American Indians in preparation for the Last Judgment. One of the first people to see the discovery of America as offering the potential for converting all the races of the world in preparation for the Apocalypse was Christopher Columbus himself. The concept was shared by most sixteenth-century Spaniards, and the obligation was taken very seriously.

Cortés's group of several hundred Europeans pitted themselves against the Aztec civilization of central Mexico which, like the ancient Romans, dominated a tribute empire extending from north of present-day Mexico City as far south as Guatemala. The heart of this realm was the city of Tenochtitlán on an island in the center of Lake Texcoco. Broad causeways linked the island to the lake shores, and giant pyramids dotted the exotic city. One of Cortés's companions, Bernal Díaz del Castillo, described his first view of the Valley of Mexico:

And when we saw all those cities and villages built in the water, and other great towns on dry land, and that straight and level causeway leading to Mexico, we were astounded. These great towns and buildings, rising from the water, all made of stone, seemed like an enchanted vision from the tale of Amadis [de Gaul]. Indeed, some of our soldiers asked whether it was not all a dream. It is not surprising therefore that I should write in this vein. It was all so wonderful that I do not know how to describe this first glimpse of things never heard of, seen or dreamed of before.

The Spanish were equally awed by the feather capes, headdresses, embroidered clothes, and gold, jade, and turquoise jewelry of the nobles. Huge pyramids were topped with temples containing carved stone and wood images of the Aztec gods with intimidating names, such as Huitzilopochtli, Tezcatlipoca, and Quetzalcoatl. The Spanish were both horrified and outraged to discover that these gods required human hearts and blood and that thousands of people were ritually sacrificed to provide sustenance for the gods.

By 1521, the conquest of Tenochtitlán was complete, with gunpowder, horses, Indian allies, and a smallpox epidemic aiding the Spanish in the defeat of the Aztec empire. Less than thirty years after Columbus discovered America, Spain had established the first Christian settlement in continental North America on the ruins of Tenochtitlán, now Mexico City. From this initial base on the continent, the Spanish branched out in all directions to conquer, colonize, and Christianize both North and South America, and ultimately the Philippine Islands, for their "God and King." By 1598, more than twenty years before the Pilgrims landed at Plymouth Rock, the Spanish had established a settlement on present-day United States soil in northern New Mexico and had reached the southern tip of South America.

Conquest and colonization in the New World were stimulated by a search for gold and souls; both were initially abundant in central Mexico. One of Cortés's first requests in his letters to King Charles I of Spain was that Franciscan missionaries be posted to New Spain with great haste to begin the enormous task of spreading Christianity to the multitude of native Americans. In 1524, the first twelve Franciscans arrived in Mexico, a number consciously chosen in imitation of the original twelve Apostles of Christ. These friars were soon followed by other Franciscans, Augustinians, Dominicans, Jesuits, secular priests, and eventually by other religious orders.

In Mexico, the friars began the mammoth tasks of converting thousands of Indians, whether by force or persuasion, establishing schools, and building churches. For many Mexican Indian tribes, such as the Maya, Mixtecs, and Tarascans, Spanish government and religion replaced those previously imposed on them by the conquering Aztecs. Many churches were constructed on the ruins of pyramids and temples as symbols of the triumph of Christianity, and pre-Hispanic gods were replaced with Christian saints. The earliest church buildings were modest and temporary. Mass baptisms were often performed in open-air chapels, but more substantial edifices were soon built.

The large fortress-like churches of sixteenth-century Mexico are reminiscent of Romanesque and Gothic religious establishments of Europe. These churches were mistakenly believed to have been the type built by the first Christians, another conscious emulation of the first age of evangelism. Most of the Mexican mission churches had long narrow naves with vaulted ceilings and polygonal apses (pl. 64). They were usually heavily buttressed and often had crenellated roof lines. The decoration was a mixture of Late Gothic, Spanish Renaissance, and Mudéjar (Moorish Christian) motifs. Interior decoration often included elaborate wall paintings in the nave and apse that were replaced by altar screens later in the sixteenth century.

Since there were few architects in New Spain, the friars had to rely on their own memory and ingenuity, along with the talents of the Indian laborers, in erecting the huge churches. Although the Mexican Indians had a long tradition of building massive pyramidal structures, there was no tradition of creating large enclosed spaces. As a result, the elaborately vaulted church structure was a completely new phenomenon to the Indians. Stone carving in pre-Hispanic Mexico was highly skilled despite the limitations of stone tools. The Indian artists quickly adapted to the metal tools introduced by the Spanish, and evidence of their virtuosity at stone carving is visible on many sixteenth-century church facades. Large churches from the sixteenth century, such as the Franciscan structure at Huejotzingo, Puebla, and the Dominican one at Yanhuitlán, Oaxaca, remain today as visible monuments to the competence of the friars and the Indians (with a few architects) and as evidence of the fervor of this age of idealistic evangelism (pl. 10, 64).

The early churches of Mexico provided a backdrop for the human drama and cultural synthesis taking place in this era of change. With the imposition of Spanish Catholicism on the local indigenous cultures of the New World, a new culture began to emerge. Aspects of European culture were transplanted to the New World where they evolved in new directions, influenced, however subtly, by native traditions and freed from the artistic strictures of Europe. Catholicism in the New World absorbed some of the native influence and displayed a unique flavor, distinctly American, with aspects that would never be found in Europe. Over the centuries the blend of Indian and Spanish elements has produced a new and distinct culture that manifests itself in the art, architecture, ritual, and traditions of Mexico.

By 1575 most of the Mexican Indians had been converted, and a series of European-introduced plagues had diminished the population. Hundreds of churches had been built, and the missionary friars were beginning to be replaced by secular priests. As a result, the late sixteenth century shifted emphasis from architecture built for conversion to decoration and embellishment of the churches. At the same time many Europeans were migrating to the New World, and the need for churches in the Spanish communities produced a new style.

In 1585 the Third Provincial Councils were held in the major cities of the New World. These councils affirmed the decisions of the mid-sixteenth-century Council of Trent in Europe and signaled the arrival of the Counter-Reformation to the New World. Cathedrals all over the Americas were renovated in preparation for this event, introducing both a purer Renaissance style and the beginnings of Baroque style for the first time. As part of the renovations, altar screens became prevalent in Mexico as the new fashion for interior church decoration (pl. 64). These early altar screens combined painting, sculpture, and architectural motifs, with narrative paintings dominating the compositions. In the tradition of the early Counter-Reformation, the large paintings emphasized didactic theology and church history.

With the discovery of silver and gold in various places in Mexico in the mid-sixteenth century, an economic boom took place. Initial rough settlements grew up around the mines and then developed into large and wealthy towns, such as Guanajuato, Zacatecas, and Taxco. The churches built in these towns in the seventeenth and eighteenth centuries were often endowed by the Spanish aristocracy and were built in the elaborate Baroque style. Parish churches were generally cruciform in plan, in conscious imitation of the shape of the Latin cross, with domes over the crossings and large belltowers (pl. 6). Altar screens were placed not only at the main altar in the apse but also at side altars lining the nave walls. These altar screens were often totally covered with gold leaf, reflecting the incredible wealth of Mexico in the seventeenth and eighteenth centuries (pl. 7).

The Baroque style in general was ultimately based on classical art but took extreme liberties by breaking up, manipulating, and multiplying classical forms. In Europe the Baroque style was particularly concerned with manipulation of space and surface. In Mexico, however, the Baroque period was characterized by extreme emphasis on the manipulation of surface with little concern for variation of space. A twisted version of a classical column, known as the salomonic, was characteristic of altar screens in Mexico during the seventeenth century (pl. 24–25). The salomonic column was popular in Europe during the Baroque period, with the most famous example being the baldachino or tabernacle built by Bernini for St. Peter's in Rome in the early seventeenth century (1624–33). Generally used with reserve in Europe, the salomonic columns seemed to multiply on Mexican altar screens and often replaced all other structural forms. Indeed, many elements of European Baroque and Renaissance art were used in extreme and inventive ways in Mexico. The Baroque style seemed to have appealed to both the Spanish and Indian sensibilities in Mexico and was carried to levels never considered in Europe.

During the seventeenth century, sculpture, rather than painting, began to dominate the altar screens, and the stories of saints and their lives began to supersede church history and dogma. The appeal of religious imagery became very direct, human, and emotional, and the desire to create a dramatic religious environment within the church began to develop (pl. 42, 59). The altar screens served as gilded backdrops and were replete with niches to showcase the images of the saints (pl. 26, 78–79). Another important aspect of the Baroque period was the theatrical use made of the light from the dome to illuminate the religious environment and symbolize the concept of heavenly light (pl. 21, 82).

In 1700, when a Bourbon grandson of France's Louis XIV assumed the throne of Spain, the lighter, more delicate motifs of French Rococo style were introduced into Spain and the New World (pl. 16). In the eighteenth century the overall design of most new churches in Mexico retained the cruciform plan and dome of seventeenth-century churches. With the renovation of the main altar of the Cathedral of Mexico, however, an important decorative motif was introduced to the Mexican Baroque style. The estípite column, which is narrower at the base and top and wider in the middle, was included in the new Altar of the Kings built by the Spanish artist Jerónimo Balbás between 1717 and 1733. The estípite column became wildly popular in Mexico and, like the salomonic column in the mid-seventeenth century, became the calling card for the eighteenth-century Mexican Baroque style (pl. 7).

In both the seventeenth and eighteenth centuries the floral decoration interspersed with cherubs that appeared on altar screens was expanded outside the boundaries of the screens and appeared on the walls of many chapels and small churches (pl. 20, 72). In the eighteenth century the altar screens further multiplied and expanded, often covering whole chapels or transepts as if they were taking over the interior space of the churches like a golden jungle (pl. 7). As can be seen in the Jesuit church of San Martín of Tepotzotlán, the Baroque concept of theatrical religious environment was carried well beyond the European interpretation to acquire a uniquely Mexican character (pl. 17, 21).

As the Baroque style spread out from the urban centers in Mexico, a stylistic evolution took place. Artistic ideas were transmitted from urban centers and from village to village in the country-side; each artist or community retained certain characteristics, discarded others, and added their own unique stamp to the end product. Artistic freedom in Mexico allowed the Baroque style to flower in new ways and to absorb a colorful and emotional character. In many remote villages, the churches can be referred to as Folk Baroque style because of their distinct and experimental variations on traditional Baroque motifs (pl. 18). In the church in the Indian village of Santa María Tonanzintla, the decorative jungle of the Baroque period has been made to cover every inch of interior space. The motifs are brightly polychromed as well as being gilded, and many of the faces of the cherubs have a darker skin tone than those in the urban churches (pl. 19).

Various regions of Mexico developed their own distinctive variations on the Baroque style, as if it had found its true home on Mexican soil where it blended with native forms and produced many hybrid combinations. In the mining towns north of Mexico City, the angular forms of the estípite style were multiplied, pleated, and folded, then covered with golden vegetation in a reflection of the mineral wealth of that region. South and east of Mexico City, in the Puebla and Oaxaca areas, the salomonic column remained popular throughout the Baroque period, and the decorative vegetation and cherubs of the altar screens were also expanded onto the church walls and facades, but here they were executed in painted and gilded stucco, rather than in gessoed and gilded wood (pl. 18–20). Brilliant facades covered with multicolored tiles became popular in Puebla, which was a major pottery- and tile-making center during the Colonial period (pl. 70–71). Farther south in the Chiapas area, and into the neighboring country of Guatemala, frequent earthquakes caused a change in the proportions of church buildings. Since it was believed that lower and wider buildings were more earthquake-resistant, the churches here were more squat in proportion, with flat facades that extended above the roof line to create the illusion of height (pl. 2–4). Called espadañas, these facades are often pierced in the upper section above the roof line and hung with bells. Espadañas were used throughout the Colonial period, first appearing on some of the sixteenth-century mission churches, and can be found as far north as the southwestern United States, but they are most common in the Chiapas-Yucatán-Guatemala area where they are often painted in bright colors to enliven the flat surfaces.

In Mexico City, a reaction against the Baroque style began as early as the 1770s, and it was decidedly replaced by the European Neo-Classical style after the opening of the Royal Academy of San Carlos in 1781. The pristine white and gold altars of the Neo-Classical style represent an international reaction against the excesses of the Baroque period and a return to the use of classical motifs in a more traditional manner (pl. 22, 68). Many Baroque churches, particularly in central Mexico, lost their extravagant gilded alter screens in this return to purist academic art (pl. 23). In more provincial areas, the Baroque sensibility of the Mexicans was not as easily suppressed, and elaborate folk variations on Baroque art continued to evolve up to the present.

The early nineteenth century saw the beginning of a struggle for independence from Spain in 1810, followed by a decade of turmoil, culminating in the founding of the Republic of Mexico in 1821. The initiator of the independence movement was Father Miguel Hidalgo y Costilla, the priest of the church of Dolores Hidalgo in Guanajuato. The rebellion began on the steps of the parish church of Dolores Hidalgo, and at the nearby church of Atotonilco the insurgent forces seized a banner of the Virgin of Guadalupe that became the symbol for the revolution (pl. 79–82). Throughout the decade of struggle, church buildings often served as refuges for troops from both sides.

The early years of the Republic of Mexico were difficult times of change and, at the same time, the Industrial Revolution was taking hold in Mexico. As part of industrial-age modernism, many older images of saints were discarded in favor of new machine-made images (pl. 52–53). Mass-produced chromolithograph prints, plaster-cast statues of saints, and Neo-Gothic wooden niches became available in Mexico from mail-order catalogs (pl. 12, 56, 62). Fresco paintings to decorate church walls, rarely used since the late sixteenth century, made a resurgence in the nineteenth century, some executed with the aid of commercial stencil patterns (pl. 41, 50, 55). Another development in religious art of the nineteenth century was that of small paintings on tin or wood, either images of saints or votive depictions of personal miracles.

In the tradition of both medieval Europe and pre-Hispanic Mexico, devout Catholics often traveled long distances to pray to a particular image of Christ or to a saint that had been credited with various miracles. The popularity of pilgrimage churches seems to have increased further in the late eighteenth and early nineteenth centuries in Mexico. The church of La Cata, built in the eighteenth century at the mouth of one of the three richest silver mines in the area of Guanajuato, lost its earlier aristocratic splendor but became one of several famous pilgrimage churches in the nineteenth century (pl. 13, 79–82). At the same time, a tradition of miracle paintings emerged, usually on small sheets of tin, depicting personal miracles accompanied by descriptions of the events in script (pl. 63). Known as ex-votos, these images, along with small silver or gold amulets (milagros) representing particular aspects of the requested or accomplished favor, were often hung in pilgrimage churches in gratitude to the responsible saint (pl. 12–13).

The churches of Mexico again served as places of refuge during the Revolution of 1910, but were sacked and damaged during those years of strife as well as during the succeeding era of strong anticlerical feeling. Regardless of prevailing political attitudes, the turmoil of civil war, and the behavior of the clergy, the churches themselves and their contents have retained their sacred places in the lives of the Mexican people through the years.

The incorporation of Christianity into Mexican life, whether initially accepted by force or desire, has become complete over the centuries. Through time, some of the more benign characteristics of the pre-Hispanic deities have been subtly transferred to the Christian saints. From the big city churches to the tiny chapels in remote villages of Mexico, the saints are regarded not as distant, transcendental beings but as intimate friends to whom the devout relate on a regular basis (pl. 47–49). This personal identification with the saints, notable throughout the Colonial period, was particularly strengthened by the emotional quality of Baroque religious art and continues today (pl. 32–33). Cofradías, or confraternities, made up of parishioners are often responsible for the care and decoration of specific images and their altars (pl. 73–74). Many individuals are drawn to a few particular saints, usually including their namesakes, and they often turn to certain images in prayer for specific problems or requests (pl. 34, 84). Both the cofradías and individuals often donate special items of clothing and jewelry along with flowers and candles to the saints (pl. 29–31). In an act of devotion, real human hair is given to make wigs for religious images, particularly of Jesus and Mary (pl. 28, 39). Sculptures with moveable arms are carefully dressed by members of the cofradías on a weekly basis and for special occasions.

In the tradition of medieval Passion plays and the Holy Week processions of Spain, large images of Christ are carried in processions at Easter in a ritual reenactment of the events of the Passion, beginning with Christ's arrival in Jerusalem on Palm Sunday and continuing through the week culminating on Good Friday with the Road to Calvary procession (pl. 36, 40). During the entire six-week period of Lent, the various saints that took part in the Passion of Christ — particularly Christ figures, the Virgin of Sorrows or Solitude, Mary Magdalen, St. Veronica, and the Disciples — are often grouped in staged scenes in churches (pl. 11, 15). Similar to Nativity scenes at

Christmas, the sculptures play the part of actors in the holy drama of Easter (pl. 57, 59). During the Lenten season, crucifixes, and occasionally entire altars, are often shrouded in purple in anticipation of mourning for Christ's sacrifice (pl. 14). Throughout the remainder of the year, the large images of Christ are usually placed on altars either in a sepulcher, holding the cross, or seated as Christ of the Cane or the Man of Sorrows, as a constant reminder of Christ's suffering for man's sins (pl. 24, 37–38).

During other religious festivals, the churches are decorated, and images of particular saints are specially clothed and taken in procession outside the church for feast days (pl. 46, 76). Amidst singing, incense, and fireworks, the saints are joyfully carried through the streets of cities and villages decorated with paper cutouts, streamers, flower petals, and greenery (pl. 30). Processions of religious images were common ritual occurrences in both pre-Hispanic Mexico and medieval Europe. In many parts of Mexico, feast day celebrations are accompanied by masked dances dating from pre-Hispanic times. These religious rituals, incorporating both European and New World traditions, demonstrate the uniquely blended character of Mexican Catholicism.

The churches of Mexico provide a glimpse of the settings in which people of all classes have lived and worshipped for centuries. They illustrate that religion was, and still is, an integral part of the lives of most Mexicans. One of the most moving experiences is to enter a church, grand or modest, on a feast day with the parishioners dressed in their finest clothes and jewels; the altars brilliant with candles, flowers, and tinsel; the air heavy with incense; and the sound of devout voices praising God in prayer or song. One is reminded that religious ritual, whether it be Christian, Buddhist, Jewish, Hindu, or pre-Hispanic Mexican, is a moving communal ceremony, whether one is a believing participant or a respectful observer. Even when the churches are empty, a feeling of cool, quiet grandeur and a sense of devotion and intimacy are present. The carefully dressed saints, lighted candles, and paper and flower decorations reflect the devotion of the community to the churches and their saints and, ultimately, to the beliefs and shared tradition they represent.

✠ *Plates* ✠

2. *Church facade, Amatenango del Valle, Chiapas.*

3. Church facade, Ocozocoautla, Chiapas.

4. *Facade of San Diego church, San Cristóbal de las Casas, Chiapas.*

5. *Church of San Jerónimo, Coatepec, Veracruz.*

6. *Church dome and bell tower, Teotitlán del Valle, Oaxaca.*

7. *Main altar, former Jesuit church of San Martín, Tepotzotlán, Mexico.*

8. *Main altar railing and prayer stools, church of Cuilapan, Oaxaca.*

9. Altar with Christ on the Cross, Instruments of the Passion and the symbols of the Four Evangelists on altar base, ranch chapel of San Miguel Viejo, near San Miguel de Allende, Guanajuato.

10. Wall mural, crucifix, Franciscan saint, and silver orb with reflection of portería (cloister entry), in former Franciscan mission church of San Miguel, Huejotzingo, Puebla.

11. *Christ in the Sepulcher, Virgin of Sorrows, and lilies during Lent, in church of Teopisca, Chiapas.*

12. *Gilded altar with Virgin and Child of the Sacred Heart (chromolithograph) and Sacred Heart with attached milagros, former Franciscan mission church of San Miguel, Huejotzingo, Puebla.*

*13. St. Anthony with ex-votos and milagros, near the entrance to the pilgrimage church of the Christ of Villaseca,
at the mouth of the famous silver mine of La Cata, Guanajuato.*

14. *Crucifix shrouded for Lent, in former Franciscan mission church of San Bernardino, Xochimilco, Mexico.*

15. *Crucifix set on purple rug with offering box during Lent, in small church near plaza, Oaxaca, Oaxaca.*

16. *Confessional with painting of Virgin of Guadalupe, former convent church of Santa Rosa de Viterbo, Querétaro, Querétaro.*

17. *Gilded angel in the vault of the camarín (dressing room) of the Virgin of Loretto attached to the former Jesuit church of San Martín, Tepotzotlán, Mexico.*

18. *Angel caryatid, church of Ocozocoautla, Chiapas.*

19. Angel caryatid, church of Santa María Tonanzintla, Puebla.

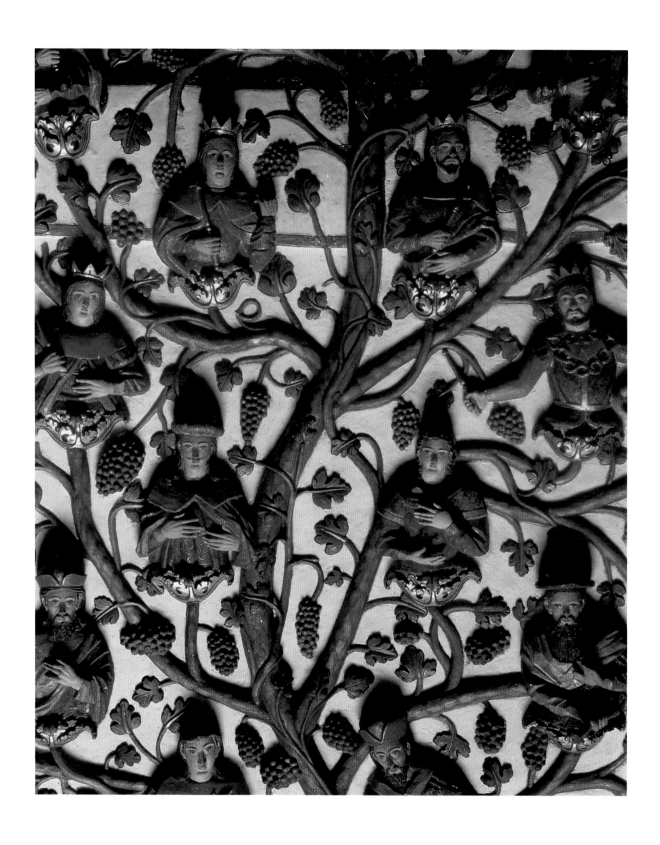

20. *Tree of Jesse of painted and gilded stucco on vault under choir loft, in former Dominican mission church of Santo Domingo, Oaxaca, Oaxaca.*

21. Cupola of camarín (dressing room) of the Virgin of Loretto, attached to the former Jesuit church of San Martín, Tepotzotlán, Mexico.

22. *Main altar with image of Virgin of Guadalupe, plaster angels, and candlesticks, in parish church of El Pichón, near Tepic, Nayarit.*

23. *Main altar, former Dominican mission church of Santo Domingo, San Cristóbal de las Casas, Chiapas.*

24. *Christ the King in altar screen niche flanked by salomonic columns with Christ in the Sepulcher below, former Dominican mission church of Santo Domingo, San Cristóbal de las Casas, Chiapas.*

25. Christ Child of Atocha, in altar screen niche, former Dominican mission church of Santo Domingo, San Cristóbal de las Casas, Chiapas.

26. Mary and Joseph in altar screen niche, former Franciscan mission church of San Miguel, Huejotzingo, Puebla.

27. Christ of the Cane in altar niche decorated with Spanish moss, small church near Yanhuitlán, Oaxaca.

28. The Virgin in wall niche, church of Santa Helena, in Santa Cruz Xoxocotlán, Oaxaca.

29. Small image of Virgin with silver crown and pearls, Templo de Jesús church, Naranja de Tapia, Michoacán.

30. Virgin and St. Anne in processional litter in church of San Bartolomé Coyotepec, Oaxaca.

31. Virgin and Child in wooden niche, church of Amatenango del Valle, Chiapas.

32. The Virgin in former Dominican mission church of St. Peter and St. Paul, Etla, Oaxaca.

33. Christ as the Man of Sorrows, former Franciscan mission church, Muna, Yucatán.

34. Virgin of the Immaculate Conception, church of Xocchel, Yucatán.

35. The Virgin of Guadalupe in sculpted and painted stone, former Augustinian mission church of St. Paul, Yuriapúndaro, Guanajuato.

36. Christ carrying the cross, in former Franciscan mission church, Izamal, Yucatán.

37. *Christ of the Cane, former Franciscan mission church of San Miguel, Huejotzingo, Puebla.*

38. *Christ of the Cane, parish church of Veracruz, Veracruz.*

39. Christ on the Cross in Templo de Jesús church, Naranja de Tapia, Michoacán.

40. *Christ entering Jerusalem on a donkey with palm leaf cross, on a litter in preparation for Palm Sunday procession, church of Matatlán, Oaxaca.*

41. Christ on the Cross in recessed alcove in church of Matatlán, Oaxaca.

42. *Saint Isidore with oxen, patron saint of farmers, in former Dominican mission church of Santo Domingo, Yanhuitlán, Oaxaca.*

43. *Skeletal image of Death, former Dominican mission church of Santo Domingo, Yanhuitlán, Oaxaca.*

44. *Soul in Purgatory in church of Patrocina María Santísima, Oaxaca, Oaxaca.*

45. *Christ of the Passion, in church of Cuilapan, Oaxaca.*

46. *Main altar, church in Cuilapan, Oaxaca.*

47. *The Virgin as the Good Shepherdess, church of Santa Cruz Xoxocotlán, Oaxaca.*

48. *Saint Joseph in the church of Santa María de Coyotepec, Oaxaca.*

49. *The Virgin as the Good Shepherdess, church of Santa María de Coyotepec, Oaxaca.*

50. Saint Michael Archangel in the church of Matatlán, Oaxaca.

51. Virgin and Child in the church of Cuilapan, Oaxaca.

52. Archangels and cherubs in storage in the cloister of former Augustinian mission of San Nicolás, Actopan, Hidalgo.

53. *Saint Justo and Saint Pastor in storage in cloister of former Augustinian mission of San Nicolás, Actopan, Hidalgo.*

54. Saint Bartholomew in church of San Bartolomé de Coyotepec, Oaxaca.

55. Altar with unidentified male saint, Christ carrying cross, and fresco of Archangels, in church of San Miguel Xochitl, Mexico.

56. *Altar with Christ as King and plaster angels in Neo-Gothic niches, former Dominican mission church of Santo Domingo, Chiapa de Corzo, Chiapas.*

57. Virgin of Sorrows, Saint John Nepomuk, and Christ of the Passion on altar in recessed alcove, church of Xocchel, Yucatán.

58. Saint Michael Archangel in church of Hoctún, Yucatán.

59. *The Pietà in altar screen niche, church of Hoctún, Yucatán.*

60. Altar niche with crucifixes and saints in ranch chapel of San Miguel Viejo near San Miguel de Allende, Guanajuato.

61. Christ on the Cross in wood and glass shrine, church of Mitla, Oaxaca.

62. Virgin of the Immaculate Conception in Neo-Gothic shrine, church of San Felipe, Oaxaca, Oaxaca.

63. *Small Christ in wooden niche with ex-votos painted on the doors, church of San Felipe, Oaxaca, Oaxaca.*

64. *Interior with main altar and side altar screens, former Dominican mission church of Santo Domingo, Yanhuitlán, Oaxaca.*

65. *Carved and gilded pulpit (R), with Saint Isidore, the patron saint of farmers, and Saint Rose of Lima, the first New World saint, former Dominican mission church of Santo Domingo, Yanhuitlán, Oaxaca.*

66. *Virgin of Solitude in painted and gilded altar niche, former Dominican mission church of Santo Domingo, Yanhuitlán, Oaxaca.*

67. Crucifix with Dark Christ in recessed niche near apse, former Dominican mission church of Santo Domingo,
Yanhuitlán, Oaxaca.

68. *Altar with the Virgin of Solitude in the church of La Soledad, Oaxaca, Oaxaca.*

69. Facade, Church of San Andrés, Cholula, Puebla.

70. *Tile facade, church of Santa María Tonanzintla, Puebla.*

71. Lamb of God on tile facade of church of San Francisco de Acatepec, Puebla.

72. *Interior of Oratorio of San Felipe Neri, San Miguel de Allende, Guanajuato.*

73. *Altar in ranch chapel, Hacienda Tirados, near San Miguel de Allende, Guanajuato.*

74. *Detail of Crucifix flanked by paintings and paper flowers on altar of ranch chapel, Hacienda Tirados, near San Miguel de Allende, Guanajuato.*

75. *Altar of Virgin of Guadalupe with modern wall paintings, church of Hoctún, Yucatán.*

76. *Interior of church with decorations, Ixtepec, Oaxaca.*

77. *Altar with Crucifix and Christ at the Column, church of Ixtepec, Oaxaca.*

78. *Dark-skinned and light-skinned images of saint in altar niche, church of Ixtepec, Oaxaca.*

79. *Unidentified female saint in altar screen niche, pilgrimage church of Atotonilco, Guanajuato.*

80. Doorway to silver chapel with fresco of a nun, pilgrimage church of Atotonilco, Guanajuato.

81. God the Father in pediment above doorway, pilgrimage church of Atotonilco, Guanajuato.

82. *Christ in Glory, suspended from vault, pilgrimage church of Atotonilco, Guanajuato.*

83. *Altar with draped cross and lithograph of Virgin of Perpetual Succor, church of Hoctún, Yucatán.*

84. Crucifix with Dark Christ, former Franciscan mission church of Muna, Yucatán.

85. Doorway to ranch chapel outbuilding, San Miguel Viejo, near San Miguel de Allende, Guanajuato.

86. *Niche with crosses and wreaths, ranch chapel, Galbones Ranch, near San Miguel de Allende, Guanajuato.*

87. *Table with crucifixes, fireworks, and wreath in ranch chapel, Hacienda Tirados, near San Miguel de Allende, Guanajuato.*

88. *Paper flower wreaths, cemetery near Mazatlán, Sinaloa.*

Designed by Eleanor Caponigro
Set in Diotima italic with Galliard by G & S Typesetters, Austin
Printed and bound by Dai Nippon Printing Company
Printed in Japan